A LOOK AT
URBAN ART

Written by
Tom Greve

Rourke
Educational Media

rourkeeducationalmedia.com

Scan for Related Titles
and Teacher Resources

www.rourkeeducationalmedia.com

PHOTO CREDITS: Cover: © Bruce Shippee (top), © kshishtof (bottom); page 1: © amdolphin; page 3: © zlisjak; page 4: © ugde; page 5: © Dmitry Pichugin; page 6-7: © Pawel Szczepanski; page 7: © Glenn Walker; page 8-9: © SeanPavonePhotol; page 10-11: © diego_cervo; page 12-13: © angi71; page 12: © DaveThomasNZ; page 13: © tirc83; page 14: © claudio zaccherini; page 15: © hsvrs; page 16: © Eric Flamant (top), © David Fowler (lower left), © Radkol (lower left); page 17: © 1000words (top left, bottom), © Radkol (top right) © Klikin (middle right); page 18: © Associated Press; page 19: © kzenon; page 20: © visith; page 21: Paul Lurrie; page 22: © Vasko

Edited by Precious McKenzie

Cover and Interior design by Tara Raymo

Library of Congress PCN Data

A Look at Urban Art / Tom Greve
 (Art and Music)
 ISBN 978-1-62169-877-7 (hard cover)
 ISBN 978-1-62169-772-5 (soft cover)
 ISBN 978-1-62169-977-4 (e-Book)
Library of Congress Control Number: 2013936786

Also Available as:

Rourke Educational Media
Printed in the United States of America,
North Mankato, Minnesota

Rourke
Educational Media

rourkeeducationalmedia.com

customerservice@rourkeeducationalmedia.com • PO Box 643328 Vero Beach, Florida 32964

TABLE OF CONTENTS

DRAWING FOR FUN

Sometimes doodling with a pencil and paper can result in interesting images.

Drawing is a basic form of artistic expression. People have been drawing throughout all of history. While the world of art goes far beyond scribbling and sketching, one style of art has gained fame for some serious scribbling, sketching, and risk-taking.

Even markings on caves from ancient times suggest humans have always had a need to express themselves through art.

Urban art is the scribbling, sketching, and painting of artistic works in the public eye. However, many urban artists create art on surfaces they do not have permission to use such as buildings, streets, or trains.

Works of urban art are usually **temporary**.

Unlike public murals where a governing body selects an artist to create something, most urban artists create their works under the cover of darkness with no pre-approval by anyone other than themselves.

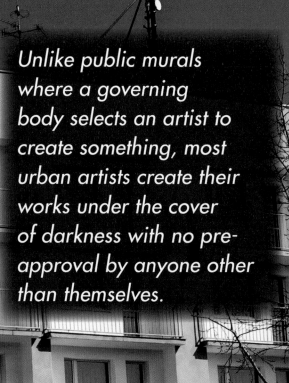

The rise of urban art has loosely followed the rise of the hip-hop music culture. Both are a reflection of life in some of the world's biggest cities.

The creation of urban art happens amid the beehive of human activity and complex spaces of big cities. Cities provide artists with **inspiration**. They also provide artists with maximum **visibility**.

The term urban art means this art is almost always created in the world's big cities. Big cities are crowded with inspiring people of diverse backgrounds.

URBAN GRAFFITI ART

One form of urban art is **graffiti**.
Street artists create their art on buildings,
billboards, or outdoor walls. Since they are
creating art while **trespassing** on someone
else's property, many street artists use false names.

The availability of spray paint and other
methods of permanent marking may have had as
much to do with the rise of graffiti as any single
person or artist.

EARLY GRAFFITI ART

Despite the risk of arrest, a teenager in New York City became one of the best-known and earliest graffiti artists back in the late 1960s. His doodles on New York City walls and sidewalks amounted to little more than his nickname, Taki, and his street address, 183.

Graffiti artists often paint on the sides of trains or subway cars so their art travels around town for greater visibility. A graffiti artist's signature style is his or her tag. Tagging is also **illegal**. Many cities treat graffiti art as a serious crime.

Chicago is the third largest city in the United States. In the 1990s, the city created a team of rapid response painters called graffiti blasters who quickly paint over any graffiti or street art that pops up around the city.

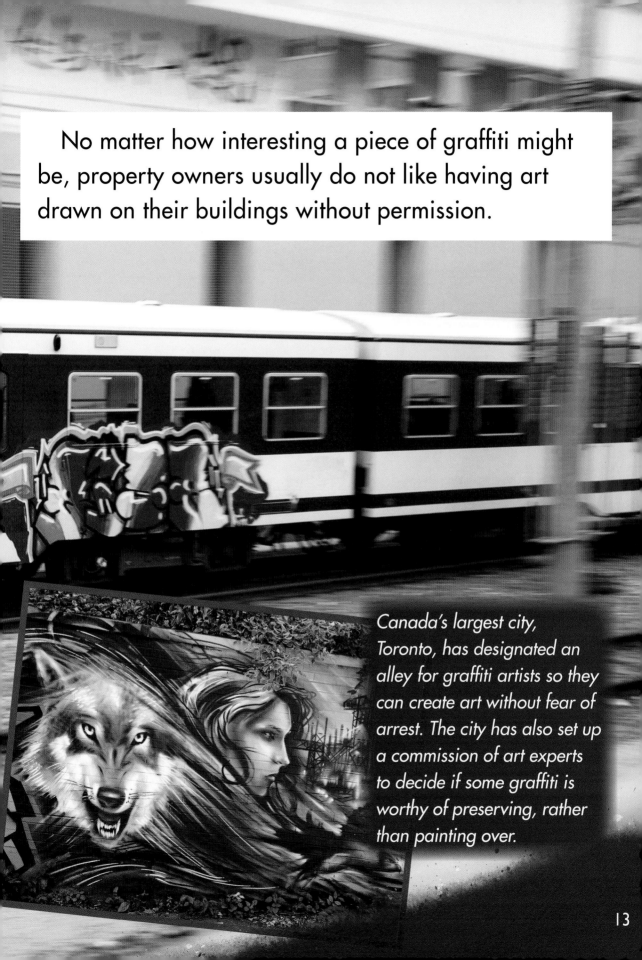

No matter how interesting a piece of graffiti might be, property owners usually do not like having art drawn on their buildings without permission.

Canada's largest city, Toronto, has designated an alley for graffiti artists so they can create art without fear of arrest. The city has also set up a commission of art experts to decide if some graffiti is worthy of preserving, rather than painting over.

URBAN STREET ART

While graffiti art involves an artistic written message, street artists draw or sketch images that may carry a message without spelling one out.

The simplicity of graffiti has influenced another urban art form known as street art. Like graffiti art, the creators of street art risk arrest to put art into the public view.

Photographs of street art, taken by admirers, keep the work alive even after the original creation is gone. Copies of these digital photos become sellable.

15

BANKSY: MYSTERY URBAN ARTIST

Perhaps the best-known street artist in the world is a British artist who goes by the name Banksy. His work has caught the eye of millions of people in cities around the globe. His art is simple but sometimes political. Like nearly all street artists, Banksy works in secrecy to avoid arrest for trespassing or vandalism.

SHEPARD FAIREY: OUT OF THE SHADOWS

Not all street artists remain **anonymous** for thier entire careers. Shepard Fairey is one of the more popular and controversial American street artists. In the 1980s his street art using an image of professional wrestler Andre the Giant with the word "obey" made him a well-known artist. More recently, he used a news photo of then presidential candidate Barack Obama to create an image titled "Hope". That image may have played a small role in Barack Obama's eventual election victory. The news organization that took the original photo later sued Fairey for using it in his art.

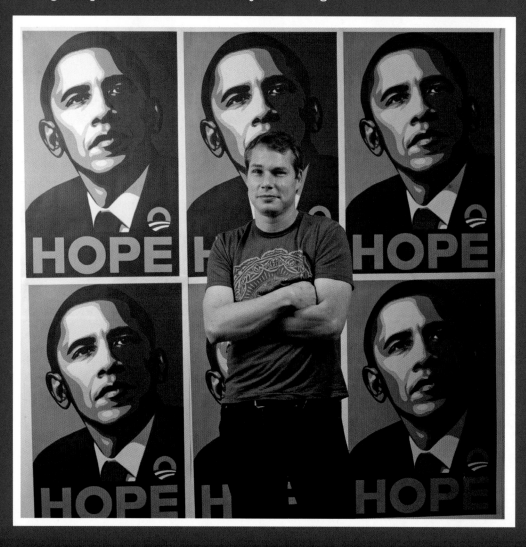

Some street art, like Shepard Fairey's, borrows images from other sources to create art with a new meaning. This repurposing of other art is popular within hip-hop music as well. Musically, it is known as sampling.

URBAN ILLUSION ART

Illusion street art often creates an appearance of depth where there is just a flat surface. Unlike more simplistic street or graffiti images, sidewalk illusion art requires more time for the artist to create a finished work.

Some artists create street or sidewalk **illusions**. These eye popping, three-dimensional drawings aim to transform everyday public spaces into dramatic optical illusions.

Modern social media has given rise to a kind of performance urban art known as flash mobs. Like graffiti and street art, these performances happen in crowded urban spaces. They form seemingly out of nowhere and then break up as quickly as they start, often to the surprise of the public.

Flash mobs organize via social media. They often appear to be silly and pointless, but they can be political.

Urban art is mysterious, inspiring, and temporary. It is also frequently illegal. Urban art is often the work of anonymous artists who are trying to get their creations seen by as many people as possible.

GLOSSARY

anonymous (uh-NON-uh-muhss): to remain unknown, or nameless

graffiti (gruh-FEE-tee): pictures or messages drawn on walls or surfaces

illegal (i-LEE-guhl): against the law

illusions (ill-LOO-zhuhnz): things that appear to exist but do not

inspiration (in-spuh-RAY-shuhn): the filling of someone with an idea to do or create something

temporary (TEM-puh-rar-ee): lasting a short time

trespassing (TRESS-pass-ing): coming onto someone else's private property without permission

urban (UHR-buhn): from or of the city

visibility (viz-uh-BILL-uh-tee): something's ability to be seen

INDEX

WEBSITES

www.CityNoise.org

www.Faso.com (Fine Arts Studio Online)

www.liv2cre8.com

ABOUT THE AUTHOR

Tom Greve lives in Chicago where he sees his share of graffiti and street art. He is married with two kids. He loves to explore the nooks and crannies of the big city on his bicycle.

Meet The Author!
www.meetREMauthors.com

24